# House Plants

Written by Karen Kenny

# TOP THAT!

Copyright © 2004 Top That Publishing plc,
Top That! Publishing, 27023 McBean Parkway, #408 Valencia, CA 91355
Top That! is a Registered Trademark of Top That! Publishing plc
www.topthatpublishing.com

# CONTENTS

# INTRODUCTION
## house plants

*Our love affair with plants stretches back centuries but the modern practice of housing plants in our homes owes much to the wealthy Victorian upper classes. As a means to impress their peers, the very rich began avidly collecting and displaying exotic fruits and plants in hot houses. Many would send out botanists with explorers to bring back new flora discovered on their journeys.*

By the late 19th century interest in indoor horticulture was growing fast and filtering down to the middle classes. Various paraphernalia was developed to encourage the use of indoor plants and it was the parlor palms, aspidistras, ferns, and plants that would tolerate low light levels which first became popular.

Gradually the working classes were able to participate in this new fashion and indoor gardening has remained a widely popular hobby ever since.

Today, house plants seem ever more important as our environment becomes more urbanized with increasing highways, car parks, shopping centers, offices and fewer green areas. Indoor plants allow us to bring greenery inside.

Recent research has found indoor foliage and other plants to be useful in removing atmospheric pollution from sealed environments and addressing the "sick building syndrome," suggesting that having and caring for house plants not only creates a pleasant environment but may bring health benefits as well!

# buying and selecting plants

Make sure you choose healthy plants which will have the best chance of survival in your home. They should also have a label with the name of the plant and the growing conditions it requires. This is useful when you are searching for a plant for a particular position.

The plant should be compact. The leaves should be firm and not limp on the stems, with good-colored foliage—no brown edges or yellowing—and no thin, weak stems with large spaces between the leaves.

Flowering plants should have plenty of buds—a greater number than flowers— and when lightly shaken few, or no, blooms should drop off. Check that the plant is not pot-bound with roots protruding through drainage holes or out of the top. If the newer leaves are smaller than the old ones this can also be an indication the plant has become pot-bound.

Make sure the compost has not dried out and shrunk away from the pot. Check the undersides of leaves, leaf nodes and the tips of new branches for signs of pests or diseases.

When taking plants home, always wrap them and let them acclimatise gradually to their new environment. Give your plants a warm bath by placing foil over the top of the pot and gently swishing the foliage through a bath of warm water with a few soap flakes added (not detergent), then rinse with fresh warm water. This will remove any

unseen insects and give the plant a good start. Water well and allow to drain for an hour.

It is natural for a plant to drop a few of its leaves as it adjusts to its new environment so do not be alarmed and do not pick off any leaves before they are ready to fall naturally. Natural leaf fall seals the point of attachment, leaving no entry point for attack from pests or diseases.

Houses are not the natural homes of plants because most will be shady and, if centrally heated, will have a dry atmosphere with fluctuating temperatures. However, there are now house plants that suit most conditions, requiring only a little attention to their needs.

When choosing your plants, find out where their native home is. Plants originating in tropical rainforests will enjoy a warm and humid atmosphere, while those from temperate regions such as the Mediterranean, China, and Japan will be happy in most houses. Desert plants are used to intermittent rain and lots of sunlight so, when caring for your plants, try to duplicate their native conditions whenever possible.

## light

Each plant requires a specific amount of light and for most this is usually bright, indirect light, so a windowsill that receives no direct light is ideal. (Remember to turn the plant regularly for even growth.)

There are many plants that can tolerate shady conditions, although some light will be required for growth. These shade-tolerant plants have dark green, chlorophyll-rich leaves. The darker the leaves the more chlorophyll they contain and the less light is needed for the process of photosynthesis to take place.

## temperature

The temperature of the average home is quite acceptable to most plants, although the drop in temperature at night can be substantial if plants are positioned on a windowsill, so it is best to remove them before closing the curtains. Sun streaming through the window, however, can scorch plants and cause them stress and they may react adversely to draughts. Giving some thought to where you position your plants can make an enormous difference to their survival.

## watering

Watering is the key to success. One of the most common threats to plants is over-watering, which can cause the roots to become waterlogged and devoid of the air which is essential to healthy root systems. In this case, little and often can be the killer. It is best to water thoroughly as the occasion demands. Water from the top unless advised otherwise, letting the water drain through the soil, then leave well alone until the next time.

Placing a large pebble on the soil is an excellent way to test a plant's water requirements. If the surface of the pebble is moist when lifted, no water is required. But if you lift the pebble and no moisture is present then that is the time to water again. Water more frequently in the summer when growth is rapid and transpiration (evaporation from the plant's leaves) takes place. Rainwater is the best water for lime-hating plants if you live in an area that has hard water.

## humidity

A dry atmosphere can easily be countered by providing each plant with its own microclimate. Place the plant on a tray of gravel or pebbles which is constantly wet, making sure the pebbles are large enough to keep the plant's base above the water. You could also use a fine mist of water from a spray bottle, but this may require moving the plants to avoid spraying nearby furniture and curtains.

## feeding

The feeding of house plants is usually undertaken in the growing season with a balanced proprietary liquid feed mixed with water, unless a special feed is required for a specific plant. Do not be tempted to use more than the recommended dose as this can lead to scorched roots and ungainly growth patterns. Newly-potted plants and young plants will not usually need feeding for six months.

# potting on and repotting

There comes a time when your plants need a change of potting soil or some extra soil for the roots to expand into.

Potting on becomes necessary when the roots are growing through the drainage holes and are matted together with little or no soil evident. Do not be tempted to pot on into an oversized pot thinking it will save work later, since your plant will take longer to acclimatize and, if it is a flowering plant, will take a very long time to return to flowering.

Choose a pot large enough to have 0.5-1 in. space all around the root ball. Lay gravel or crocks (broken clay pots) over the drainage holes and then a layer of fresh compost so that the roots will be covered with 0.5 in. of soil—this should allow enough room for watering, but the amount should be equal to one-seventh of the total pot depth so vary accordingly.

Remove the plant from its pot by placing your hand across the top of the soil with the stem between the first and middle fingers. Turn the pot upside down and tap gently against a hard surface. Tease out any roots which have begun to spiral and trim away one-third if they are excessively coiled.

Place in a new pot in fresh compost, then carefully pour potting soil around the sides and press down with your fingertips, lightly but firmly.

Repotting should only be done when the plant is dormant and is a good way of controlling the growth of plants such as shrubs and climbers and for bulbs, corms and tubers. Simply remove from the pot and shake off the old potting mix. A hand fork can be used for bigger shrubs and climbers. Trim the roots, removing about one-third to a half of the root system, and then repot in the same sized pot with some fresh compost.

Proprietary composts sold for house plants are ideally balanced and devoid of disease and weeds. The type of compost needed for each plant should be indicated in its cultivation notes.

## pots

Clay pots are preferred by many people because they are porous and allow air to move in and out. However, they tend to dry out, so plants will need watering more frequently. Plastic pots do not dry out so rapidly but as long as the compost is of a good quality, plants do equally well in either type. These may then be placed in ornamental ceramic pots to blend with your décor or stood on saucers to catch excess water.

## shaping and cleaning

Prune large plants to maintain their shape; pinch out tips of shoots to control height and produce bushy plants. Pinch just above a leaf joint or node—start when plants are no more than 6 in. tall and repeat the process regularly.

Should you want to produce a "standard plant"—a myrtle, for example—allow it to grow to the required height, removing branches from the main stem as it gets taller. When the required height is reached, begin pinching out to produce the standard "lollipop" shape. Rotate your plants to keep them growing symmetrically.

Use a leaf shine mitt to remove everyday dust and, from time to time, wash foliage using pure water and a soft sponge—sponge the underside of the leaves too, because this will often help to control red spider mite on plants.

## propagation

There are many methods of propagating plants. Some of the easier methods are covered in this section for you to try out. Use a well-draining, water-retentive medium to start off your cuttings: vermiculite, perlite, or a good grade of sand all work well. Take your cuttings from healthy plants only. Humidity is often essential in propagating and it is useful to store cuttings in clear plastic bags until they have rooted and show signs of new growth. Remember, however, to ventilate regularly to prevent rot.

**TERMINAL CUTTINGS** are taken from the growing point of the stem with one or two nodes below. Make a cutting, using a sharp blade, 3-5 in. long, trim the leaves from the base and insert into the medium of your choice.

**LEAF CUTTINGS** are varied. Single leaf cuttings of sansevieria, for example, are simply inserted into the medium in 3 in. sections and will root.

**LEAF BUD CUTTINGS** should use a piece of stem that has one or two nodes along its length. The stem is then laid on the medium and will root from the nodes.

**LEAF PETIOLE CUTTINGS** consist of a stem with a leaf attached. The stem is inserted into the medium where a plantlet will form.

**DIVISION OF PLANTS** is simple and is often used for ferns as well as aspidistras. Remove the plant from its pot and cut through the rhizomes, or root stalks, with two or more growing points to each section. Plant in pots of a suitable medium and water thoroughly.

**RUNNERS** have almost ready-made plants waiting on the ends of the runners to be planted. Pot them while they're still attached to the "mother" plant, and when rooted, cut from the main plant.

**OFFSETS** are easy. Just pull or twist the offset from the base of the main plant and pot. Similarly, suckers of a good size will grow readily when broken off at the base of the plant with a few roots of their own. Just pop them in a pot with a suitable medium.

**TUBERS AND RHIZOMES** such as the caladiums can be propagated by division of the tuber when new shoot growth occurs. Each section should have a bud or an eye; dry overnight and then pot.

# FLOWERING

## flowering house plants

*There is so much pleasure to be derived from cultivating and nurturing flowering house plants into bloom. The wonderful perfumes, the delightful colors and the shapes of both the flowers and foliage, enhance our living space, creating interesting and pleasant environments. According to feng shui, flowers represent romance and placing flowering plants in the bedroom by your wedding photograph bodes well for a lasting and happy relationship! Flowering plants may also help to bring wealth if you place three plants with round leaves, and red or purple flowers, together in the left-hand corner of your room.*

# lipstick vine/royal red bugler

*An epiphytic (non-parasitic plant which uses another as its host) hanging basket plant from Java.*

◆ **Appearance:** Glossy, deep green, elliptical leaves. Clusters of crimson, tubular, hooded flowers each 1.5 in. long with purple-brown calyx borne at the tips of branches in spring. Before they open, the flower buds are dusky red tubes with protruding red petals, giving the appearance of the top of a lipstick!

◆ **Height and spread:** 18-24 in.

◆ **Compost:** Proprietary peat-based compost, well drained.

◆ **Location:** Bright light, screened from direct sunlight in the summer.

◆ **Temperature:** High humidity in the summer months, syringe frequently in hot weather. Night temperature around 55°F (13°C), will survive at 45°F (7°C) if kept dry in the winter.

◆ **Water and feed:** Water regularly, keeping compost moist but not wet. Liquid feed every 21 days during spring and summer. Water very sparingly in the winter months. Repot every three years in the spring.

◆ **Propagation:** Take 2 in. tip cuttings of non-flowering shoots in May. Layering by pegging down in moist compost from April to July.

# flamingo flower/tailflower

*An exotic plant with colorful spathes and dark green leaves, from Central and South America.*

◆ **Appearance:** Brilliant scarlet, waxy, palette-shaped spathes, 3-4 in. in size, with a spiral orange-red spadix. The spathes will last a month or more and will "flower" from spring right through to fall. The cut flowers are often used for floral arrangements.

◆ **Height and spread:** 9 in. spread, 12-15 in. high, with lanceolate leaves dark green in color, growing up to 7 in. long.

◆ **Compost:** Half sphagnum moss, half potting mix, well drained (fill pots with one-third of drainage material). Keep growing points clear of compost.

◆ **Location:** Medium light levels. North-facing window in the summer; east or west in the winter.

◆ **Temperature:** Likes high humidity so keep on a bed of pebbles. Requires a constant temperature of around 65°F (20°C); minimum winter temperature of 50°F (10°C).

◆ **Water and feed:** Water moderately from October to March. Keep moist, but not wet, during the growing season. Add liquid feed every fourteen days from May to August. Repot every three years in the spring.

◆ **Propagation:** Divide in March or April, retaining a growing point on each piece. Pot in compost and keep in humid conditions until established.

## poinsettia

*A deciduous plant from Mexico and Central America that's popular at Christmas.*

**Appearance:** The "flowers" consist of colorful, elliptical leaves called bracts. The true yellow and green flowers in the center of the bracts are borne from November to February. The familiar and colorful bracts may be crimson or scarlet, and even pink and white forms are also available.

◆ **Height and spread:** They can be 3.3-4.9 ft high and spread 6-20 in., with elliptical bright green leaves shallowly lobed.

◆ **Compost:** Proprietary peat-based.

◆ **Location:** Bright, indirect light: a minimum of six hours bright light daily to survive. In summer, from June onwards, it may be put outside in a sunny sheltered position until September.

By the end of September you will have a sturdy plant; that is the time to encourage the bracts to change color. To achieve this place the plant in a black bin liner at around 6 pm and remove it at 8 am the next morning, ensuring a total blackout for fourteen hours daily for around eight weeks; then bring the plant into a well-lit position away from draughts. After "flowering," when the leaves fall naturally, move to a shady, cool position until potting on in May.

◆ **Temperature:** Warm temperature minimum of 70°F (16°C) during growing season, after "flowering" reduce to 50°F (10°C).

◆ **Water and feed:** Water regularly during the growing season, allowing the top of the compost to dry out between waterings. When the leaves have fallen naturally, cut the plant back to 3 in. above the compost and keep almost dry until the first weeks in May when you should replant in the next size pot. Water copiously the first time and then regularly, as before. Keep the plant warm to encourage new shoots, pruning to the strongest five shoots. Use weak liquid feed at 7-10 day intervals from June to September.

◆ **Propagation:** Stem cuttings from the prunings in May. Keep at a temperature of 21°C (70°F) until well rooted.

## african violet

*A tender, evergreen perennial, this native of Central and East Africa has become one of the most popular house plants over the years.*

◆ **Appearance:** Single purple flowers, produced in small umbels throughout the year, 1-2 in. across, violet-like with round petals.

◆ **Height and spread:** They grow to 3-4in. and spread 6-9 in. The mid- to deep-green leaves are almost heart-shaped, with a velvety texture. There are hundreds of cultivars available with differing leaf shapes and flower colors, some double flowered, and there are even miniature saintpaulias.

◆ **Compost:** Proprietary peat-based.

◆ **Location:** Position in moderate light, away from direct sunlight.

◆ **Temperature:** They thrive in warm, humid atmospheres— 65-70°F (18-21°C)—but will tolerate temperatures as low as 60°F (16°C).

◆ **Water and feed:** Overwatering can be fatal. Keep the compost moist, but not wet, at all

times, standing on a bed of pebbles. Keep water off the leaves to avoid marking them. Watering from below with capillary action is often the best method. Using tepid water, set the pot in a pan of water and as soon as moisture is seen on the surface of the compost remove and drain. Give specialist saintpaulia liquid feed at ten- to fourteen-day intervals.

◆ **Propagation:** Take leaf cuttings with around 2 in. of stalk between June and September, insert singly into 2.5 in. pots, at a temperature of 64-70°F (18-21°C). Plantlets will form at the base of the stem. When large enough, plant into individual pots. Continue to pot on as the plant grows until it is in a 4 in. pot. Repot established plants at two-year intervals to maintain vitality.

## cape jasmine

*This evergreen shrub from southern China is a challenge to keep as a house plant as considerable care is needed to maintain it. However, its beautiful, large, fragrant, white flowers make it well worth the effort.*

Gardenia Jasinoides Veitchiana responds to the same treatment.

◆ **Appearance:** *Gardenia Jasinoides Fortuniana* flowers in summer. White, waxy blooms, 3 in. across, with a fabulous heady perfume, are borne in the leaf axils of the tops of the shoots. The dark, glossy, green, lanceolate leaves are an excellent foil for the pure white flowers.

◆ **Height and spread:** It can reach just over 3 feet, but the size can be controlled by pinching out the growing tips. The similar winter flowering

◆ **Compost:** Proprietary peat-based.

◆ **Location:** Good, bright light is essential for flowering. The plant will need at least four hours of light daily, but shade from direct sunlight in summer. Avoid draughts.

◆ **Temperature:** Keep warm, between 60-70°F (16-21°C) for most of the year. Night

temperature is crucial to flowering and should be around 62-65°F (17-19°C). Above this temperature you will have more vegetative growth at the expense of flower buds and increased bud drop. Winter temperature for summer flowering plants is around 54°F (12°C).

◆ **Water and feed:** Water regularly with pure water, allowing the top of the compost only to dry out between applications. Both over-watering and under watering will cause bud drop, as will any sudden change in temperature. Liquid feed at 10-14-day intervals during the summer. In winter, slow down the watering of summer-flowering plants, just keeping them moist. Water winter-flowering varieties freely during the winter months.

◆ **Propagation:** Cuttings of young shoots, preferably with a heel, should be taken in spring and kept at a temperature of 60-70°F (16-21°C). Pinch out the tips of the shoots after flowering and thin any non-flowering growth.

# FOLIAGE
## foliage plants

*The wonderful architectural structure of many foliage plants lends itself to interior design. The myriad of colors that may be found in the stems and leaves of foliage plants—from the caladium's pinks and reds, to the deep green of the aspidistra leaves and the creams of variegated plants—add light and interest to a dark and dull corner. Some varieties can be great fun, such as the maranta which closes its "hands" in prayer as it "goes to sleep" in the evening. In feng shui it is suggested that we put healthy plants in as many rooms as possible to generate positive energy.*

# angel's-wings/elephant's-ears

*An outstanding foliage plant from the hot and humid Amazon Basin.*

◆ **Appearance:** The large, arrowhead-shaped leaves come in various colors including red, pink, green, and cream. White and silver are often a combination in each leaf. The leaves are of an almost translucent crepe-like texture. Caladiums can be enjoyed at all times of the year as the growth period is determined by the start of the growth cycle. Any flowers that may appear should be removed to maintain the quality of the foliage.

◆ **Height and spread:** 12-24 in. high, the caladium spreads to 12-24 in. also.

◆ **Compost:** Proprietary peat mixture, good drainage is essential.

◆ **Location:** Place in bright, indirect light in a warm room, avoiding draughts, which are fatal to caladiums.

◆ **Temperature:** High humidity at an even temperature of around 70-80°F (20-23°C); keep on a bed of pebbles. Store dormant tubers at 55-60°F (14-16°C).

◆ **Water and feed:** Keep compost moist with regular watering; allow the surface of the compost to dry out between applications.

Add half-strength liquid feed at 10-14-day intervals during the growing season. As the leaves start to wither, reduce watering until the tuber is dormant. Store in pots and water lightly once a month to keep soil barely moist.

◆ **Propagation:** Use offsets of small tubers at repotting time. If the tuber is large, divide the tuber with each portion having an "eye." To encourage a tuber into growth after a rest period of at least four months, remove old compost and small tubers. Pot each tuber into an appropriate-sized pot, placing the tubers at a depth equal to their size. Keep compost just moist and at a temperature of 70°F (21°C) until the roots are well developed and the foliage is emerging. Then treat as normal.

# aluminum plant

*From Southeast Asia its common name of aluminum plant is derived from its silver-gray markings, which give the leaves the appearance of aluminum. These are, in fact, air spaces between the tissues of the leaves.*

◆ **Appearance:** Leaves are quilted, ovate, dark green with the silvery patches up to 3 in. long and grow in pairs alternating along the stem.

◆ **Height and spread:** Up to 12 in.; small, brown flowers may appear on the tips of the stems. *Pilea Cadierei "Nana"* is more compact.

◆ **Compost:** Proprietary peat mix, with good drainage.

◆ **Location:** Bright light away from direct sunlight in summer. Plants will tolerate up to 40 percent of shade.

◆ **Temperature:** Warm, between 64-70°F (18-21°C) during summer; will tolerate higher temperatures as long as humidity is kept high. Stand on a bed of pebbles. Winter temperature should range from 55-60°F (13-16°C).

◆ **Water and feed:** Water freely during the growing season, allowing the top of the compost to dry out between intervals; use the pebble test as a guide. Add liquid feed at half strength at 14-21 day intervals. Water sparingly in winter.

◆ **Propagation:** Take 3-4 in. long stem cuttings in spring and summer at a temperature of 64-70°F (18-21°C). Pot on as roots form and to correspond with the plant's growth. Repot mature plants each spring.

# sensitive plant/humble plant

*Although this tropical American plant has flowers, it is usually grown as an annual for its delightful foliage.*

◆ **Appearance:** The light green, bipinnate leaves made up of numerous elliptical leaflets give the plant its common name. If touched during daylight they are very sensitive and fold together with even the leaf stalks bending, hence they are "humble" and very sensitive. They will resume their prevous state if left alone for a short period. The small, pink, tufted, globe-shaped flowers, about 1 in. in diameter, appear in leaf axils in July and August.

◆ **Height and spread:** They can reach up to 24 in.

◆ **Compost:** Proprietary soil-based or peat mix.

◆ **Location:** Requires a good light source, such as a sunny windowsill with light shading in the summer months. Keep humidity high and stand on a pebble bed.

◆ **Temperature:** Keep warm, 64-70°F (18-21°C), with high humidity to ensure a happy and thriving plant.

◆ **Water and feed:** Water regularly, keeping the plant moist but not soggy; dryness causes leaf drop. Liquid feed at half strength at fourteen-day intervals during the summer.

◆ **Propagation:** Sow seeds in February or March, in seed compost at a temperature of 64-70°F (18-21°C). Pot on as necessary until in the final pot.

## classic or common myrtle

*This Mediterranean, tender, evergreen shrub has long been associated with love and peace and is often included in wedding bouquets*

◆ **Appearance:** A compact, bushy plant with glossy, mid to dark green, ovate, aromatic leaves. Small white flowers in summer are sometimes followed by purple fruits. Variegata has creamy white variegations on the leaves and is very attractive.

◆ **Height and spread:** As a pot plant of 24-35 in., it can be trained as a "lollipop" standard.

◆ **Compost:** Proprietary peat mix.

◆ **Location:** Direct light. Plants can be stood outside during the summer.

◆ **Temperature:** Cool to warm, 45-55°F (7-13°C) with a winter temperature of 41°F (5°C).

◆ **Water and feed:** Water freely as needed in the summer with rain or lime-free water. Keep compost moist in winter. Liquid feed (lime-free) at fourteen-day intervals from May to September.

◆ **Propagation:** Use 2-3 in. cuttings of non-flowering, lateral shoots, preferably with a heel in June and July, at a temperature of 61°F (16°C). When well rooted, pot on and pinch out the tips to bush out. Once established, repot every other year in spring and shear annually in spring to maintain shape.

## prayer plant/rabbit's tracks

*This fascinating plant from Brazil has the wonderful habit of closing its leaves like hands in prayer when in darkness, hence its common name, and the blotches between the veins resemble rabbits' tracks.*

◆ **Appearance:** A prostate plant with large, ovate leaves. The young leaves are a bright emerald green with brownish blotches between the herringbone veins. As they mature, the leaves become a gray-green with darker blotches. The new leaves are tightly rolled and protrude at the ends of the stems.

◆ **Height and spread:** Grows up to 6-10 in. high with a spread of 12 in. or more. Large plants are particularly good in hanging baskets.

◆ **Compost:** Proprietary peat or soil-based mix.

◆ **Location:** Medium light, ideally on an east- or west-facing window on a pebble bed.

◆ **Temperature:** Keep warm and humid during winter at 55-70°F (13-18°C).

◆ **Water and feed:** Water freely during the summer with tepid, lime-free water. Water moderately during the winter. Liquid feed at fourteen-day intervals from May to September.

◆ **Propagation:** The rhizomes may be divided and replanted in the spring. Alternatively, take basal cuttings with two or three leaves, keep at a temperature of 70°F (21°C) until roots have formed, then pot on and treat as mature plants. Marantas are rapid growers and need repotting annually. Trim old straggly growth to keep them tidy.

# cast iron plant

*From China, the aspidistra has the reputation of being the most enduring of plants if neglected. It will tolerate gas fumes, low light and extremes of temperature and dryness.*

◆ **Appearance:** Long, dark green, lanceolate leaves can reach 20 in. or more narrowing to a stalk. *Aspidistra Elator "variegata"* has cream-striped leaves and is very attractive. The cup-shaped, purple-brown flowers are unusual, growing at soil level in August on mature plants.

◆ **Height and spread:** This plant reaches a height of 24-30 in., also spreading to 24-30 in.

◆ **Compost:** Proprietary peat mix.

◆ **Location:** Light shade, by a north-facing window during summer. Plants should receive no direct sunlight at all.

◆ **Temperature:** Ideal range of 45-50°F (7-10°C) but will tolerate short periods at lower temperatures, and up to 80°F (28°C).

◆ **Water and feed:** Water freely in the summer, keeping the soil moist, but not soggy, and with some humidity. It will, however, tolerate dry air. Needs less water in the winter. Sponge leaves occasionally to keep them clean. Feed at 21-28 day intervals with weak liquid feed during the summer.

◆ **Propagation:** Divide and replant each section with at least two or three leaves in the spring. Aspidistras like to be pot-bound, so repot every second or third year. If larger plants are required, pot on each spring until in the required size pot. Ten-inch pots give a good-sized aspidistra.

# SUCCULENTS
## succulents

Succulents tend to come from arid or semi-arid climates so they are well adapted to tolerate such conditions. This has meant the changing of physiological structures such as the reduction of the surface area of the plants, shallow rooting habits and modification of the stomata to reduce the loss of fluid. Succulents usually have fleshy, soft, thickened stems, leaves and tubers, enabling them to store fluid in case of drought.

## flaming katy

*A small shrub from Madagascar, it gives a delightful, colorful display in the winter months.*

◆ **Appearance:** Mid-green, fleshy, ovate leaves with scalloped edges. Masses of four petalled, 0.5-1 in. tubular flowers in various shades of red. Newer varieties now include yellow, white and pink. The flowers are borne in dense, flat-headed clusters on stems rising from the leaf axils.

◆ **Height and spread:** Approximately 12 in.

◆ **Compost:** Proprietary soil-based or peat mix.

◆ **Location:** Bright light. Position on a sunny windowsill. It needs at least half a day of sunlight each day, especially in the winter.

◆ **Temperature:** Warm; 50-55°F (10-13°C), or less for winter flowering. Higher temperatures minimize flowering.

◆ **Water and feed:** Water regularly in the summer, allowing the top of the compost to dry between applications. Keep moist in the winter. Liquid feed at 21-28 day intervals.

◆ **Propagation:** Take 3-4 in. stem cuttings in May to August; allow to dry for two days before potting up at a temperature of 65°F (18°C). Sow seeds on the surface of seed compost at a temperature of 70°F (21°C); prick off when large enough to handle and pot on as necessary. Repot mature plants each spring.

## century plant

*A splendid plant from Mexico and Central America.*

◆ **Compost:** Proprietary soil mix with added sand.

◆ **Location:** Sunny, airy position, outside in the summer, shaded from the midday sun.

◆ **Temperature:** Although said to be cold-tolerant it is best kept above 41°F (5°C) in winter.

◆ **Water and feed:** Keep dry in winter, adding only enough water to prevent shrivelling. Gradually increase in spring and summer, allowing drying out between watering. After the first year feed with a potassium-rich fertilizer when watering in the summer.

◆ **Propagation:** Basal rosettes known as "pups" can be potted up after drying out for several days. Will also grow successfully from seed. Repot every two or three years.

◆ **Appearance:** Rosette forming rigid, grey-green leaves with prickly edges and needle-sharp pointed tips. Known as the century plant because of its slow growing habit and production of long stemmed flowering spike several feet high with many paired green tubular flowers appearing between 15 and 50 years. After the effort of flowering, it then dies.

◆ **Height and spread :** 4 ft when outside but remains compact when potted.

# jellybean plant/many-fingers plant

*From Mexico, a tender dwarf succulent with club or jellybean-shaped fleshy, grayish green leaves, with a light, waxy coating and reddish tinged ends.*

◆ **Appearance:** Flat clusters of yellow flowers, about 2-3 in. across, appear in spring.

◆ **Height and spread:** 10-12 in.

◆ **Compost:** Soil-based, with extra grit and sand added. Do not use a rich compost or the leaves will become rank and only a few flowers will be produced.

◆ **Location:** Full light and sun with good ventilation. Move outside in the summer months.

◆ **Temperature:** Winter temperatures should not fall below 41°F (5°C).

◆ **Water and feed:** Allow the top couple of inches of soil to dry between watering. Water less frequently in winter allowing the top two-thirds of the soil to dry out in between times. Dilute liquid feed to one-third strength and add at 28-day intervals during the growing season.

◆ **Propagation:** Place leaf cuttings face down on a bed of sand, keep moist and pot plantlets individually as they appear.

# partridge-breasted aloe

*A native plant of South Africa.*

**Appearance:** The dark green leaves are marked with white irregular bands with white-toothed edges. The leaves are arranged in three overlapping ranks forming a rosette-like appearance. Upright spikes of tubular orange flowers appear in spring.

**Height and spread:** Up to 8 in. height and 15 in. spread according to pot size.

**Compost:** Soil-based.

**Location:** The dry air of a sunny windowsill suits this plant admirably, although a light shading during midsummer is advisable. It can be stood outside in the summer.

**Temperature:** Minimum temperature of 41°F (5°C) in winter; 45-50°F (7-10°C) is ideal.

**Water and feed:** Water freely from late spring to early fall to keep moist but not ever wet. Over-watering is fatal so it's better to be on the dry side of moist. Water less in the winter and spring, keeping almost dry. Never allow water into the rosette. Dilute liquid feed to half strength at 28-day intervals during the growing season.

**Propagation:** Take offsets from the mother plant during summer severed with a knife with some roots attached. Allow to dry for 24 hours then set in soil-based compost, with the leaf bases just on the surface and anchored with pebbles. Repot mature plants annually in spring, again anchoring the plants with a covering of pebbles.

## string of beads

*An excellent indoor hanging basket*

*plant from Southwest Africa.*

◆ **Appearance:** Matt-forming plant with creeping stems and glaucous, globular, fleshy green leaves resembling small grapes, each one having a translucent vertical band. It has scented, white daisy-like flowers with purple stigmas on 2 in. stems that appear from September to November.

◆ **Height and spread:** Spreading 2 in. and growing up to 24-35 in. high.

◆ **Compost:** Soil-based with extra grit added.

◆ **Location:** A sunny position hanging in a window basket.

◆ **Temperature:** Minimum winter temperature of 50°F (10°C).

◆ **Water and feed:** Water freely during the growing season allowing the top half an inch to dry out in between watering. Keep compost just moist during winter. Feed at half-strength twice during the growing season.

◆ **Propagation:** Set stem cuttings, taken from spring to fall, in a compost of half peat and half sand.

# living stones/pebble plant

*These amazing plants from South Africa use disguise as their defense mechanism. To stop them being eaten by animals, they look like pebbles on the ground.*

◆ **Appearance:** Small plants consisting of two thickened, mottled leaves joined to form an un-branched body with a slit across the top. Colors are mainly gray-green to reddish brown. Being part of the mesembryanthemum family, they produce daisy-like, yellow or white flowers from the split. The stems of these plants are buried in the soil and the leaves have a "window," which allows the light to penetrate down to the assimilating tissue.

◆ **Height and spread:** Growing to about 1-2 in. maximum.

◆ **Compost:** Soil-based mixed with equal amounts of sand or grit.

◆ **Location:** Position in full sun for 4-5 hours in the morning and partial shade in the afternoon in an airy location. After winter, acclimatise to full sun over a short period.

◆ **Temperature:** Minimum temperature of 41°F (5°C) in winter, but 45-50°F (7-10°C) is ideal. Lithops can withstand high temperatures in the summer.

◆ **Water and feed:** In summer, the plants become dormant, saving as much water as they can by closing down and resting. At this time they require only sufficient water to survive and prevent shrivelling, too much and they will rot. Water just the top half inch of soil. They begin their growth cycle in fall so a good drenching of water around the middle of August will encourage this process. Drain well and from then on allow the soil to almost dry out between watering intervals.

The center of the plant will throw out a bud, which will become the flower, after which watering should be decreased. By late September the plant should be dried out

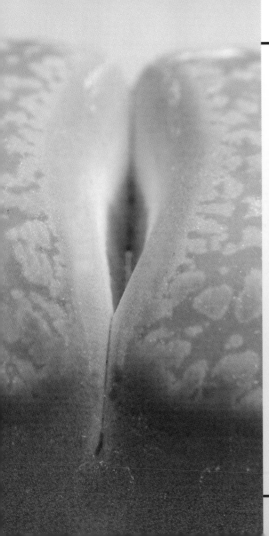

completely. After the flowering is over a new pair of leaves will be seen forming.

Do not be tempted to water when you see the old leaves begin to shrivel, as the new ones are drawing the water and nutrients from these in order to grow. When the old leaves are completely shrivelled they may be removed and watering can commence again, gradually increasing as the plant grows.

By mid-spring, full watering will be in order; use a drench and draining procedure, allowing the soil to dry in-between. By late spring gradually reduce watering ready for the summer dormancy. No feed is usually necessary.

◆ **Propagation:** Sow seeds on the surface of seed compost in spring at a temperature of 70°F (21°C) and pot up. Clump-forming species can be divided by removing a plant body with the stem attached. Dry out for three or four days and pot into growing medium. Repot plants every two to three years.

# jade plant/money tree

*This South African, tree-like succulent originally gained its common name of "money tree" because of its feel of coins and, because if neglected too much, a windfall would leave the plant bare. Now it is felt that while the plant thrives so will the fortunes of the household. However, should it be neglected then your fortunes will also decline! According to feng shui it is wise to keep plants with round leaves that look like coins in the left-hand corner of as many rooms as possible to ensure wealth in the home!*

◆ **Appearance:** Tree-like trunk with branches bearing bright jade green, obovate, fleshy leaves with a kind of silvery scale, edged in red in the sunlight. Mature plants will reward you with clusters of star-shaped, white flowers at the tips of branches. Be patient since they can take up to seven years before flowering.

◆ **Height and spread:** The size of the plant is controlled by the dimensions of the pot and pinching out.

◆ **Compost:** Proprietary soil-based.

◆ **Location:** Position in full sun to partial shade all year. Too little light will make the stems thin and prone to breaking. May be stood outside in the summer.

◆ **Temperature:** Winter temperatures should not drop below 41°F (5°C) 45-50°F (7-10°C) is ideal. During summer it can withstand high temperatures but prefers 65-80°F (18-24°C).

◆ **Water and feed:** As with most succulents, little or no water is required throughout the year. Over-watering is their biggest enemy. Only water when the soil becomes dry and seldom in winter. Feed mature plants at half-strength once every three months.

◆ **Propagation:** Leaf or stem cuttings will root easily in moist sand. Repot mature plants every second year in the spring.

# cacti

*True cacti must exhibit a number of characteristics. As part of the succulent group of plants they have also developed distended fleshy stems of various shapes, which carry out the functions of leaves, which are rarely found in cacti. As perennials, they produce seeds with two cotyledons and the fruit is a berry enclosing the seeds. Areoles or spine cushions are also always present, although the spines are sometimes replaced with fine hairs which are barbed at the ends (glochids); the petals of the flower rise from the top of the fruit.*

*When repotting cacti, it is advisable to wear gloves, and another good tip is to wrap the cactus in newspaper as you remove it from the pot.*

## bunny ears/polka dot cactus/prickly pear

*From Mexico, the opuntia is perhaps the best known of the cactus family, with its flattened oval stems resembling bunny ears.*

◆ **Appearance:** Pale green with deep yellow glochids, which can easily break off and penetrate the skin, so careful handling is required. The lemon-yellow flowers that bloom in early summer, are 1-2 in. in diameter and the resulting fruit, containing the seeds, is usually red or purple. It does not often flower and fruit as a house plant. The dormant period is important to all cacti, especially if you want them to flower.

◆ **Height and spread:** Will grow up to a metre in height when potted on into larger and larger pots.

◆ **Compost:** Proprietary cactus compost, or soil-based compost.

◆ **Location:** Light, airy position with plenty of sunlight.

◆ **Temperature:** A winter temperature of no less than 45°F (7°C).

◆ **Water and feed:** Not as succulent as some cacti. Light watering is required during the summer to keep the compost just moist. Water very sparingly in the winter—only enough to stop the soil drying out completely.

◆ **Propagation:** Take cuttings in summer and allow to dry slightly for two to three days then pot into soil with added sand, where they will easily root. Repot mature plants annually in spring.

## rat's tail cactus

*This epiphytic cactus from Mexico will grow well in a basket.*

◆ **Appearance:** Has a profusion of wonderful funnel-shaped, magenta-colored flowers which last up to five days and measure from 1-3 in. long. These form along the stems during spring and are followed by small red fruits.

◆ **Height and spread:** Eight to twelve ribbed, mid-green, 0.5 in. thick stems, with short spines, grow up to 35 in. long. The stems grow draped over the edge of a pot or basket.

◆ **Compost:** Proprietary soil-based.

◆ **Location:** Sunny position in a dry atmosphere.

◆ **Temperature:** Will tolerate high summer temperatures with some protection from the afternoon sun. Winter temperature of 41°F (5°C) is necessary in the dormant period to ensure flowering.

◆ **Water and feed:** Water regularly in the summer during the growing period, allowing compost to dry out between watering. Liquid feed with high potassium at fourteen-day intervals during the summer. Reduce watering in the winter to a minimum to keep the soil just moist.

◆ **Propagation:** Stem cuttings between April and July. Allow to dry off for two to three days and pot into compost with added sand. Repot mature plants annually after flowering.

# old man cactus/mexican old man

*Another fabulous cactus from Mexico. The long, white hairs, or spines, act as a sunscreen and, by trapping air next to the cactus, help to cool the plant in the hot summer sun. It is these long white hairs that give it the common name of old man cactus.*

◆ **Appearance:** Nocturnally flowering with pink flowers during the summer.

◆ **Height and spread:** This is a slow-growing pillar cactus, which in its native habitat can grow to 8-35 in; however, pot size will keep it under control.

◆ **Compost:** Proprietary cactus or soil-based, with extra grit added.

◆ **Location:** Dry, full sun, away from draughts.

◆ **Temperature:** Tolerates high summer temperatures with some protection from the afternoon sun. Optimum winter temperature is 41°F (5°C).

◆ **Water and feed:** Regular spring and summer watering, allowing soil to dry between watering again. Dry during dormant period from November to February. Add half-strength feed at 28-day intervals from May to August.

◆ **Propagation:** Take stem cuttings and allow to dry out for two to three days and pot into compost. Sow seeds in spring at a temperature of 70°F (21°C). Repot mature plants every two years.

# gherkin cactus/peanut cactus

*It is the clusters of pale green, finger-sized stems with white bristles looking for all the world like green peanuts or gherkins that give this cactus its common names.*

◆ **Appearance:** An excellent first cactus to grow as it will flower from an early age, giving a good display of vivid orange-red or yellow flowers, 2 in. in diameter, in the spring.

◆ **Height and spread:** Easy to cultivate, it grows to a height of 6 in. and spreads to 12 in.

◆ **Compost:** Proprietary cactus or soil-based, with extra grit.

◆ **Location:** Choose a sunny position with a dry atmosphere.

◆ **Temperature:** Winter temperatures should not fall below 41°F (5°C), or rise above 60°F (16°C).

◆ **Water and feed:** Regular spring and summer watering, drying soil out between watering again. Liquid feed at half-strength from April to August at 28-day intervals. Water sparingly in winter, just to prevent any shrivelling of the plant.

◆ **Propagation:** Take offset stems, drying before planting in compost with added sand. Repot every second year.

# hedge cactus

*From Argentina and Brazil; mature plants will reward you with scented, funnel-shaped white flowers in June and July which open at night. Each blossom lasts just one night, so don't miss it.*

◆ **Appearance:** A columnar, upright blue-green branching cactus with six to eight flat ribs. It sports five to ten spines in clusters at areoles.

◆ **Height and spread:** Can grow up to 52 ft in its native habitat, but can be controlled with pot size and cutting back.

◆ **Compost:** Proprietary soil-based with added grit.

◆ **Location:** Sunny position.

◆ **Temperature:** Winter temperatures should not fall below 41°F (5°C).

◆ **Water and feed:** Apply plenty of water in the summer while the plant is growing, allow to drain thoroughly but leave till almost dry before watering again. In winter, keep dry, just preventing shrivelling.

◆ **Propagation:** In spring or early summer, to control the growth of this plant should it become too tall, cut off the top 12 in. Allow to dry for a week and then pot up into a sandy compost. The original stem will send out branches from the cut surface. Stem cuttings taken from the branches of 3-4 in., left to dry for two to three days and potted up in the same way will increase your stock. Repot annually in spring.

# FERNS

ferns

*Ferns grow in almost all parts of the world. Beautiful foliage plants, they need shady places to grow. Ferns are known as cryptograms as they do not produce flowers or seeds but spores on the undersides of their fronds.*

To collect spores, use a plain piece of white paper and fold into it a mature frond with spore heaps beginning to turn brown. In a few days the spores will have been released in the form of a "dust."

Propagate by placing a tiny sample of the spores on top of a previously sterilized and glass-covered seed compost. Replace the glass as soon as you have placed the spores. Leave in a shady greenhouse and be patient. Four to twelve weeks later, a green film of prothalli will appear (these are heart-shaped growths having both male and female organs). Keep the glass in place and water from below, keeping the compost just moist.

As they grow, prick them out into a tray of compost and keep in a closed atmosphere. Small fronds will begin to appear when they're large enough to plant into individual pots. Ferns can also be propagated by division, which is an easier and quicker way to produce mature plants, but spore propagation is a greater challenge.

# maidenhair fern

*From Brazil, this delicate plant has pale green, triangular fronds, which bend over gracefully as they mature.*

◆ **Appearance:** The fronds are made up of many small pinnules (the leaflets forming the fronds) on thin, black-purple stalks.

◆ **Height and spread:** This fern grows up to 15-24 in. high with a spread of 12-18 in.

◆ **Compost:** Proprietary peat mix with added sand.

◆ **Location:** A humid atmosphere is essential to the wellbeing of this plant, so place on a pebble bed away from direct sunlight.

◆ **Temperature:** Needs warm temperatures, with a minimum winter temperature of 50°F (10°C). It will withstand high temperatures provided there is also high humidity. Mist during the hot summer months to increase humidity.

◆ **Water and feed:** Water regularly in the growing season from March to August, keeping compost moist but not soggy. Reduce water in the fall but do not allow to dry out. Add half-strength liquid feed at 28-day intervals through the growing season.

◆ **Propagation:** Divide in spring, crocking pots well to ensure good drainage. Cut fronds of mature plants as they turn yellow. Repot mature plants at the end of March. To revitalize old plants occasionally cut off all fronds when repotting; new growth will emerge after a couple of months. It is also possible to propagate from spores.

# bird's nest fern

*Its common name derives from its tropical Asian habitat where it grows as an epiphyte and looks like a bird's nest clinging to the trees.*

◆ **Appearance:** An attractive fern, producing a rosette of lance-shaped, shiny green, stiff fronds with a blackish-colored midrib and wavy margins.

◆ **Height and spread:** Can grow up to 3 ft.

◆ **Compost:** Proprietary peat or soil mix.

◆ **Location:** Indirect light from an east- or west-facing window; avoid south-facing positions. Stand on a pebble bed. Can be stood outside during summer in a shady position.

◆ **Temperature:** Enjoys cool night temperatures of around 50-55°F (10-13°C). Daytime temperature should be between 60-70°F (15-21°C) throughout the year.

◆ **Water and feed:** Water regularly during summer, keeping compost moist but not soggy. Reduce water in the fall, but do not allow soil to dry out completely. Feed with half-strength liquid fertilizer at 30-day intervals during summer.

◆ **Propagation:** Spores germinate easily. Repot every other year in the spring, making sure the plant is set at the same depth as before.

# PTERIS ENSIFORMIS "VICTORIAE"

# silver table fern/variegated sword brake

*This cultivated variety of* pteris ensiformis *originates in the Himalayas through to Australia.*

◆ **Appearance:** The slender green leaflets have a white midrib.

◆ **Height and spread:** Slender stems, some arched barren fronds, and some erect fertile fronds give a height of 18 in. and spread of at least 12 in.

◆ **Compost:** Proprietary peat mix with added sand.

◆ **Location:** Indirect sunlight from a window, not south-facing. Stand on a pebble bed. Can be placed outside in summer.

◆ **Temperature:** Ideal temperature range is 60-85°F (16-29°C); winter temperatures should not fall below 55°F (13°C).

◆ **Water and feed:** Water regularly during the summer, keeping compost moist but not soggy. Reduce water in the fall but do not allow the soil to dry out completely. Feed with half-strength liquid feed at monthly intervals during the summer.

◆ **Propagation:** In April, divide plant or sow spores at 55°F (13°C). This fern will give fast- growing plants from spores. Repot plants every other spring.

## asparagus fern

*Although not strictly a fern, this is an excellent foliage plant from Natal, frequently used in floral arrangements and in hanging baskets.*

◆ **Location:** Well-lit position out of direct sunlight.

◆ **Temperature:** Winter temperature should not fall below 45°F (7°C).

◆ **Water and feed:** Water regularly in the summer, reducing amounts in the fall but keeping the compost slightly moist. Liquid feed at fourteen-day intervals during the summer.

◆ **Propagation:** Divide in spring, or sow seeds during April at a temperature of 61°F (16°C) and plant in seed compost. Repot mature plants annually in spring. As phyllocades turn yellow remove stems from the base to encourage new growth.

◆ **Appearance:** The long, arching stems with hooked prickles bear masses of stiff, yellow-green, needle-like phyllocades (a flattened stem functioning as a leaf). On mature plants, small greenish-white flowers may appear in June, followed by small red globular berries.

◆ **Height and spread:** Up to 12 in. high and a spread of about 3 ft.

◆ **Compost:** Proprietary peat mix.

## staghorn fern

*This fabulous, unusual epiphytic plant comes from tropical areas of Australia, New Guinea and Indonesia.*

◆ **Appearance:** They normally grow on trees and have two types of fronds. Wavy-edged, pale green fronds, aging to tan, lie flat at the base of the plant and serve to support and gather organic matter to help feed the plant. The mid-green, forked, upright, fronds are fertile and bear the spores near their tips. The close resemblance to deer antlers explains their common name. They may also be grown in hanging baskets.

◆ **Height and spread:** 18-24 in.

◆ **Compost:** Requires sphagnum moss when grown on slabs of bark. In hanging baskets, use a mix of two-one-one by volume, fibrous peat—sphagnum moss—fibrous loam, making sure there are plenty of crocks for good drainage.

◆ **Location:** Partial shading, around 55 percent shade.

◆ **Temperature:** Keep warm; 60-85°F (16-29°C). Winter temperatures should be above 50°F (10°C).

◆ **Water and feed:** Mature plants require water every four days during the growing season and only sufficient amounts to stop the fronds wilting in winter. Use half-strength liquid feed at monthly intervals during the summer.

◆ **Propagation:** Propagate by division from February to March: cut with a sharp knife, keeping a good piece of the rhizome with each section. Attach to a fresh bark slab, over a handful of moss, with chicken wire. Water and mist daily to keep humidity levels high. When new growth is seen, water at intervals of three days and feed at half strength weekly until well established. Then treat as for mature plants. Propagation by spores is also possible.

# boston fern

*These popular rhizomatous ferns*

*from the tropics are easy to grow.*

◆ **Appearance:** Wide-spreading pinnate (feather-like) fronds, mid to dark green in color, arch gracefully, making this plant ideal in baskets.

◆ **Height and spread:** Fronds may measure up to 20 in.

◆ **Compost:** Proprietary peat mix.

◆ **Location:** Indirect sunlight from a window, not south-facing. Pebble bed.

◆ **Temperature:** Ranging from 50-73°F (10-23°C), with winter temperatures above 50°F (10°C).

◆ **Water and feed:** Water regularly in the summer, allowing compost to be moist but not soggy. Reduce amounts in the fall to keep the compost just moist.

Boston ferns can benefit from extra humidity during the summer with regular misting using lime-free water. Add half-strength feed at fourteen-day intervals during the summer growing season.

◆ **Propagation:** Propagate from spore or divide the plant in the spring, setting young clumps in equal parts of peat and sand at 55°F (13°C).

# palms

*Palms are those wonderful plants that remind us of exotic places. In their natural state they will be found in areas of high humidity, with warm temperatures, good air circulation and space to grow.*

For these plants to be successful in the house it's often necessary to replicate these conditions as accurately as possible. There are some palms, however, that are quite tolerant and, with care, will live happily in the home.

Good drainage is important to all palms, so well-crocked pots are in order. Humidity is provided by plunging the potted plant into a larger planter with a good pebble bed and the sides filled with peat moss. Many will have low light requirements, which is a bonus. Misting with lime-free water in the heat of summer ensures high humidity. Occasional sponging of the leaves to remove dust is also necessary for the wellbeing of these graceful plants.

# parlor palm/good luck palm/dwarf mountain palm

*Originating from Mexico, this is one of the easiest palms to cultivate. It is a single-stemmed plant with arching pinnate leaves of narrow, dark green leaflets.*

◆ **Appearance:** Panicles (flower heads with several branches either opposite or alternate) of tiny yellow flowers are followed by tiny, whitish berries, resembling pearls which may appear on mature plants providing the plant receives sufficient light.

◆ **Height and spread:** A slow growing palm, reaching no more than 3.9 ft.

◆ **Compost:** Proprietary soil-based peat mix.

◆ **Location:** Can thrive in a shady position but locating in bright, indirect light is best. Requires good winter light.

◆ **Temperature:** Keep at 60-85°F (16-29°C), with a winter temperature above 50°F (10°C).

◆ **Water and feed:** Water regularly in the summer, keeping soil moist but not soggy; mist to increase humidity with lime-free, tepid water. In winter keep soil just moist. Liquid feed monthly from April through to September.

◆ **Propagation:** Sow seeds in spring at a temperature of 75°F (24°C); pot on when two or three leaves have developed. Two or three plants are often planted together in the same pot to give a good display.

# sago palm

*Although not a true palm as such, this native of Japan is technically a cycad, a group of plants dating back to before the dinosaurs!*

*As a cone-bearing plant it requires both the male and female plants in order to produce seeds.*

◆ **Appearance:** Slow-growing, with feather-like, green leaves growing in a circular pattern giving it a tropical palm-like appearance.

◆ **Height and spread:** Its leaves grow outward forming 24-35 in. circles. Can grow to 10 ft high over time.

◆ **Compost:** Proprietary peat mix with added sand.

◆ **Location:** Full sun is preferable but the sago palm is very adaptable and will grow indoors as long as it has several hours of bright light each day.

◆ **Temperature:** Extremely tolerant with a temperature range of 15-108°F (11-42°C).

◆ **Water and feed:** When the soil is almost dry water thoroughly. May require weekly watering during hot spells but wait until light levels are low. Water every few weeks at other temperatures. Feed during the summer with half-strength liquid fertilizer.

◆ **Propagation:** Offsets or "pups" grow at the base and may be removed and potted up after drying for several days. Plant in well-drained, sandy soil with half the ball below soil level; water thoroughly. Allow soil almost to dry out between watering. After several months the new leaves will start to appear. Allow the new plant to form a good root system before potting on. Sago palms like to be root bound and may remain in the same pot for many years.

# chinese fan palm/fountain palm

*This fabulous palm from Australia has large, glossy green, fan-shaped leaves. The single trunk will eventually become quite large and outgrow the house!*

◆ **Appearance:** The leaves are deeply divided with long, drooping tips, giving it the appearance of a fountain. The stems are covered with "teeth."

◆ **Height and spread:** As young plants these lovely palms will give several years of enjoyment before having to move on to larger homes.

◆ **Compost:** Proprietary peat or soil-based.

◆ **Location:** Full sun to partial shade; ensure good light through the winter months. Position outside in the summer.

◆ **Temperature:** A range of 60-75°F (16-24°C) is best, but the fountain palm will tolerate a lower winter temperature 50°F (10°C).

◆ **Water and feed:** During the growing season, water soil well, allow to drain and leave to dry to 1 in. below the surface between watering. Reduce watering during the winter rest period. Feed monthly during the growing season with half-strength fertilizer.

◆ **Propagation:** Sow seeds in moist peat in spring.

# pygmy date palm

*A native of Laos and Vietnam its slow growth makes it ideal as a house plant.*

◆ **Appearance:** Delicate-looking, soft, flat, green fronds rise from a central crown.

◆ **Height and spread:** Will eventually grow to around 7-10 ft, according to pot size.

◆ **Compost:** Proprietary peat or soil mix.

◆ **Location:** Indirect sunlight, outside in summer in dappled shade, a good light source in winter. Pebble bed.

◆ **Temperature:** Keep in a temperature range of 16-82°F (16-28°C); will tolerate lower winter temperature of around 50°F (10°C).

◆ **Water and feed:** Keep the soil moist during summer and feed half-strength liquid fertilizer at weekly intervals. Reduce watering during the winter period.

◆ **Propagation:** Remove offsets from the base and pot up during spring. Regularly sponge the leaves.

## coconut palm

*This is a fun plant to grow and keep for a few years. A young coconut palm sprouting with half of the seed exposed will be a good talking point, and clearly demonstrates how this plant came to populate various islands as it was washed ashore and grew where it lay.*

◆ **Appearance:** The glossy, feathery fronds of the coconut are a familiar sight, reminiscent of magnificent white, sandy beaches.

◆ **Height and spread:** As with other palms, the coconut palm will eventually outgrow the house.

◆ **Compost:** Proprietary peat-based with added sand.

◆ **Location:** Indirect sunlight. Place outside in summer and locate near a good light source in the winter.

◆ **Temperature:** Keep within a temperature range of 60-82°F (16-28°C).

◆ **Water and feed:** Drench and drain, allow partial drying between watering. Add half-strength liquid feed at fourteen-day intervals in the summer.

◆ **Propagation:** A hit-and-miss process but certainly fun; the freshest nuts are most likely to succeed, as this nut was washed ashore after traveling for a while and was still able to germinate, so it could for us too. Plant and cover three-quarters of the nut in moist, sandy, peat-based compost, keeping warm and moist at all times, then just wait. It can take up to six months to germinate and when it does, what a sense of achievement! Keep the seedling in bright sunshine and the compost moist until it is well established.

# BROMELIADS
## bromeliads

*This fascinating collection of plants ranges*

*from Spanish moss* (Tillandsia usneoides)

*which used to be used as a stuffing for*

*upholstery, to the delicious pineapple*

(Ananas comosus).

They have a varied lifestyle with some choosing to live in bright sunlight on sandy beaches, and some on rocks sending their roots into cracks in the rock faces. Others are epiphytic and live on host plants, gathering moisture and nutrients from the air.

They all have small scales on their "leaves" called trichomes (plant hairs, scales or bristles growing from the epidermis rather than from inner tissue). In arid areas these serve to reduce water loss and protect from the sun's rays and may appear white and hairy.

All bromeliads have a rosette-like arrangement of leaves with a central cup; in some epiphytic species the cup is where water collects as well as the occasional insect and leaf debris which becomes the main moisture and food reservoir. To encourage flowering, place an apple with the bromeliad in a clear plastic bag. The apple releases ethylene gas which will induce the plant to flower.

# urn plant/silver vase plant

*Originating from Brazil, it is the best known of all the bromeliads and can be said to be the "signature" plant. Although an epiphyte in its natural state, it may be grown in soil as a house plant.*

◆ **Appearance:** The strap-like, gray-green leaves with black spines are banded with silver scales to form a cup from where the amazing flower head will emerge. The flower head, reaching up to 6 in. long, appears in August and is made up of a mass of pink-spined bracts which last for several months. Tubular blue flowers gradually turning rose-pink emerge from between these bracts. When the flowering is over and the bracts begin to fade the plant will seem poorly; however, side shoots will form to replace the mother plant.

◆ **Height and spread:** The plant reaches up to 24 in.

◆ **Compost:** Proprietary bromeliad mix or any open-textured lime-free mix.

◆ **Location:** Good light with partial shade during the summer months. Keep on a pebble bed.

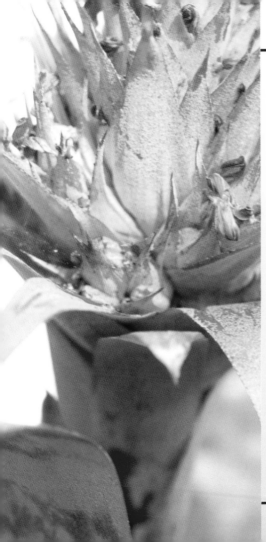

◆ **Temperature:** Keep warm at temperatures ranging from 55-65°F (13-18°C); avoid temperatures lower than 50°F (10°C) in the winter.

◆ **Water and feed:** The compost should be kept just moist in summer and barely moist in winter. The main watering is through the rosette or cup in the center of the plant; keep this filled with tepid, lime-free water from late spring to early fall, and just moist during the winter period. Misting will help to maintain a humid atmosphere during summer.

◆ **Propagation:** Take offshoots from the base of the plant when they reach one-third of the size of the mother plant. Sever with a sharp knife, dry for 24 hours, then pot up into the same compost as the mature plant and stake until rooted firmly. Top-dress the mature plants with an annual top dressing.

## flaming sword

*This plant from Guyana produces a flower spike of bracts reminiscent of a flaming sword, from which yellow flowers emerge in late summer, which last for several months.*

◆ **Appearance:** Complementing the colorful flower are strap-like, dark green leaves, with purple-brown banding.

◆ **Height and spread:** Grows up to 18 in. high.

◆ **Compost:** Proprietary bromeliad mix, or half sand, half-leaf mold, or osmunda fiber.

◆ **Location:** Partial shade with high humidity. Stand on a pebble bed.

◆ **Temperature:** Optimum temperature range of 65-70°F (18-21°C); winter temperatures should be around 60°F (16°C).

◆ **Water and feed:** Water the compost regularly during summer, allowing it to become almost dry between applications and keep the rosette filled with water from April to September. In winter, reduce water to keep compost and rosette just moist. Mist with lime-free water during the summer to increase humidity.

◆ **Propagation:** Take rooted offsets in the spring when they reach half the size of the mother plant. Allow to dry for a couple of days, then pot in the same mix as the parent plant. Repot mature plants every two to three years in the spring.

## pink quill

*From Ecuador, this beautiful plant is epiphytic but can easily be grown in a pot.*

◆ **Appearance:** The linear channelled leaves, reddish brown at the base with brown vertical lines, form the rosette. The half-hidden flower stem has a 3.5 in. high, 2.5 in. across, blunt spike of tightly overlapping pink bracts with three-petaled, violet-colored flowers that emerge in ones and twos.

◆ **Height and spread:** Reaching a height of 9 in. and spreading to 12 in.

◆ **Compost:** Proprietary bromeliad mix, or half sand, half leaf mold, or osmunda fiber.

◆ **Location:** Sunlight; partial shade during the summer months. On a pebble bed.

◆ **Temperature:** Thrives in warm temperatures of 55-65°F (13-18°C); avoid temperatures lower than 50°F (10°C) in the winter.

◆ **Water and feed:** Water the compost regularly in summer, allowing the compost almost to dry out between watering. Keep the rosette filled with water from April to September. In winter, reduce water to keep compost and rosette just moist. Mist with lime-free water during the summer to increase humidity.

◆ **Propagation:** Take rooted offsets in the spring when they reach half the size of the mother plant. Allow to dry for a couple of days and then pot in same mix as parent at 60-70°F (16-21°C). Repot mature plants annually in spring.

# blushing bromeliad/painted lady

*A popular plant from Brazil with strap-like, bright green leaves with ivory stripes that flatten out to pointed tips—the true beauty of this plant is in the leaves, which change color as the plant flowers.*

◆ **Appearance:** When flowering is about to occur the leaves turn a wonderful shade of pink that is concentrated at the center; this coloring will last until the plant declines. The flower head arises from the central rosette in a rounded sessile (stalkless) cluster. The violet-colored flowers open one to three at a time.

◆ **Height and spread:** Grows to 12 in. high with a spread of 24 in.

◆ **Compost:** Proprietary bromeliad mix.

◆ **Location:** Sunlight in partial shade will ensure good colored leaves and encourage flowering. Stand on a pebble bed.

◆ **Temperature:** Keep warm at 55-65°F (13-18°C), avoiding temperatures lower than 50°F (10°C) in winter.

◆ **Water and feed:** Water the compost regularly in summer, allowing the soil to become almost dry between watering. Keep the rosette filled with water from April to September. Reduce water to keep compost and rosette just moist in winter.

◆ **Propagation:** Use offshoots from the base of the plant with the roots attached. In June, sever with a sharp knife, pot up into the same compost as the mature plant and stake until rooted firmly. Keep plantlets in a humid atmosphere until well rooted. Repot mature plants every three to four years in spring.

## queen's tears/angel's tears

*A tropical American plant whose graceful arching habit makes it ideal for hanging baskets.*

◆ **Appearance:** Long, narrow and serrated leaves, dark green in color with a silvery-bronze tint, arch together to form the rosette. The 0.5-1.5 in. long, green tubular flowers with reflex petals, edged with violet and showing yellow stamens, emerge in long, branching clusters of pink bracts.

◆ **Height and spread:** Grows up to 18 in.

◆ **Compost:** Any open-textured, lime-free mix.

◆ **Location:** Good light away from direct sunlight. Stand on a pebble bed.

◆ **Temperature:** Keep warm at temperatures from 55-65°F (13-18°C), although the plant can endure very low temperatures, down to 38°F (3°C), for short spells.

◆ **Water and feed:** Water the compost regularly in summer, allowing it almost to dry out between watering. Keep the rosette filled with water from April to September. Reduce water to keep the compost and rosette just moist in winter. Mist with lime-free water during the summer to increase humidity. Feed with very diluted quarter-strength liquid feed during the growing period.

◆ **Propagation:** Take offsets in June to July when they reach half the size of the parent plant. Allow to dry for a couple of days, then pot in the same mix as the parent plant and stake until firmly rooted. Repot mature plants annually in June.

## spanish moss

*This amazing epiphytic bromeliad from South America is often seen hanging from trees in meter-long festoons. In the past it was used as stuffing for mattresses. It is a delight to grow as it requires scant attention, no repotting or feeding, just regular misting with tepid water and a warm environment.*

◆ **Appearance:** Long, wiry strands of moss-like tufts with tiny, linear, scaly, grey leaves. The inconspicuous yellow-green flowers are borne in leaf axils through spring and early summer, although these are rarely seen in cultivation.

◆ **Height and spread:** Grows to 10-20 in.

◆ **Compost:** This plant requires no compost; attach directly to twigs, bark slabs or even enameled wire.

◆ **Location:** A moist, humid atmosphere is important, with plenty of good light.

◆ **Temperature:** Optimum temperature range of 68-75°F (20-24°C) in summer, but will tolerate higher temperatures. Keep temperature around 60°F (16°C) in winter.

◆ **Water and feed:** Regular misting with tepid water is all that this plant requires, taking traces of nutrients from the air.

◆ **Propagation:** Remove a few shoots or plantlets and hang on bark slabs to start all over again.

# FRUITING PLANTS

Have you ever looked in your fruit basket and wondered what the plants they came from look like? Well, why not have some fun and have a go at growing some? You could be pleasantly surprised, and think of the sense of achievement when visitors ask where you got such a lovely plant from.

The following are just some of the fruiting plants that you can grow well with just a little care.

## avocado/alligator pear

*Originating from the warmth of North and South America, as a house plant the shiny foliage will offer much enjoyment.*

◆ **Appearance:** Alternate elliptical shiny, dark green leaves with paler veining on branches from the main stem. The flowers of a mature tree appear in January in panicles of small, yellow-green flowers.

◆ **Height and spread:** The growth of this plant should be controlled by the size of the pot.

◆ **Compost:** Proprietary soil or peat-based with a little added sand.

◆ **Location:** Requires several hours of good light each day. Can be put outside during the summer.

◆ **Temperature:** Keep warm at temperatures ranging from 61-75°F (16-24°C). In winter ensure the temperature is above 50°F (10°C).

◆ **Water and feed:** Keep compost moist but not soggy, and well drained. Water less in the winter months. Feed monthly during the summer.

◆ **Propagation:** A common method is to use three toothpicks inserted into the stone of the fruit suspended over a jar of water. This method, however, is liable to knocks and spills—an easier alternative places the stone directly onto the compost. Keep the stone half exposed, the compost moist but not waterlogged, and cover the entire pot with a plastic bag, maintaining the temperature at around 70-75°F (20-25°C).

In a while the stone will split and a shoot emerge. The roots form first so, although it may look as if nothing is happening, don't be disheartened as it can take from two to at least six weeks to emerge. When the stem reaches 6-8 in. cut back to half its size to encourage branching. Regularly pinch out the tips to make a nice bushy plant. Pot on until it is in a 10 in. pot, then repot every two years in spring.

# pineapple

*Coming from tropical America, the pineapple is a typical bromeliad with all their corresponding characteristics.*

◆ **Appearance:** It has a rosette of pointed, strap-like, gray-green serrated leaves which can reach 35-60 in. across. It bears fruit on a stalk from the center of the rosette. The stalk is short and carries lavender-blue, three-petaled flowers which fuse with the bracts to form the delicious fleshy fruit we all know and enjoy.

◆ **Height and spread:** Grows and spreads to 3.2-6.5 ft.

◆ **Compost:** Proprietary soil or peat-based with added sand.

◆ **Location:** Good light; at least one hour of good light each day. Humidity should be kept high so stand on a pebble bed.

◆ **Temperature:** Keep warm, 68-77°F (20-25°C). In winter, keep temperatures above 61°F (16°C). Can be stood outside in summer in dappled shade.

◆ **Water and feed:** Keep moist, allowing the top inch to dry out between watering. Feed using half-strength liquid feed at fourteen-day intervals during the summer. Mist regularly to increase humidity.

◆ **Propagation:** After enjoying this delicious fruit cut the top with at least 1.5 in. of fruit. Remove the fleshy bit to reveal the central core—this is the original flower stalk. Then carefully remove the lower layers of leaves until you see some small bumps (these will become the roots).

Leave the hard core of the fruit to dry off for a day or two, then plant in damp, very sandy, compost. Place in a light, warm position in a large plastic bag to retain humidity and spray regularly. A temperature of 74°F (23°C) bottom heat will encourage the roots to grow. Pot on into final compost after roots are well formed—usually around four to six weeks. When at least two years old it should be ready to flower and to encourage this place in a large plastic bag with an apple. The apple will produce ethylene gas, which will encourage flowering, as it does with other bromeliads.

# coffee plant

*The coffee plant, with its origins in Ethiopia, is an evergreen shrub with opposite pairs of elliptical shiny, dark green leaves, sometimes 6 in. long.*

◆ **Appearance:** Large plants will produce five-petaled, pure white, fragrant flowers, borne in clusters in the leaf axils during late summer. Half-inch-long oval, crimson berries develop, each of which when ripe contain two coffee beans.

◆ **Height and spread:** The coffee plant can grow to 3-6 ft and with a spread of 2-4 ft. However, for use as a house plant, judicious pruning and pot size will maintain an appropriate size and shape.

◆ **Compost:** Proprietary peat compost.

◆ **Location:** Requires good light but it should be screened from direct sunlight in midsummer to avoid the leaves being scorched.

◆ **Temperature:** Best suited to temperatures of 16-24°C (61-75°F); keep the room temperature above 12°C (54°F) in winter.

◆ **Water and feed:** Keep soil moist but not soggy through the growing period from March to October; the soil should be drier in the winter months. Mist during summer when the temperature goes above 61°F (16°C). Add liquid feed at fourteen-day intervals during the summer and monthly during the winter.

◆ **Propagation:** A fresh, unroasted coffee bean sown in a seed compost and kept warm and humid will eventually germinate and produce beautiful coppery-colored, small leaves which gradually change to a glossy, dark green as they mature.

Cut out the top growth to promote branching. They will not flower and fruit until at least three to four years old, but are well worth the wait. Give the roots plenty of room in large pots. Prune mature plants by cutting back the previous year's growth by two thirds each spring to control growth. Stem tip cuttings may be taken in summer from upright branches and provided with a bottom heat of 70-75°F (21-24°C).

## pomegranate

From the Mediterranean region, pomegranates are a great fruit when you're young and have competitions as to how far you can reach with your pips! So the next time the children are competing why not "salvage" some of the already "cleaned" pips and sow them. The resulting tree will be a pleasure and a talking piece.

◆ **Appearance:** Slow growing with oblong, shiny, mid-green leaves. The flowers, borne singly or sometimes in clusters, are bright scarlet from June to September. The yellow-orange fruits contain many seeds surrounded by fleshy sweet pulp. *Punica granatum "nana"* is a dwarf form of pomegranate, which will also bear fruit.

◆ **Height and spread:** The pomegranate plant will grow 8-10 ft feet high, and spread 5-8 ft.

◆ **Compost:** Soil based.

◆ **Location:** Full sunlight especially in winter with good ventilation.

◆ **Temperature:** Warm 61-75°F (16-24°C) winter temperature best above 54°F (12°C).

◆ **Water and feed:** Water regularly, keeping soil moist, but not soggy, with good drainage.

Reduce water during the fall months and maintain at just moist during winter. Add half-strength liquid feed monthly during the summer.

◆ **Propagation:** Sow fresh seeds, minus pulp, in March in a soil-based seed compost at 60°F (16°C). Pot on as they grow until in 10 in. pots. By this time, however, they will have outgrown the house and should be moved into a greenhouse or gradually acclimatized to life outside in areas where the temperature does not drop below 41-45°F (5-7°C). Repot every other year in spring. *Punica granatum "nana"* may be purchased, and makes an excellent house plant from which seeds may also be grown.

# PLANT PROBLEMS

## plant problems

The most important tool any gardener has, whether outside or inside, is their eyes. Observation of all of your house plants will alert you to any problems early and allow you to take the necessary action to rectify the situation.

Watering is the ideal time to make your inspection: make sure you look at the underside as well as the tops of all the leaves; it is the undersides most insects tend to favor. A magnifying lens will help you to identify the culprits. Washing is usually the simplest and most environmentally friendly way of eliminating pests. Hand-pick any larger pests that you may encounter in the summer months when many of your plants may be enjoying a period outside.

If you find a serious problem on a single branch, judicious pruning may be all that is needed, although a follow-up of washing the rest of the plant is advised. Should you return from a period away from home to discover your plant seriously infested then it is often wise to discard the plant as it will be severely stressed and vulnerable to attack from diseases.

Plants well looked after will seldom suffer from diseases; however, observation will enable you to remove any infected part of your plant in the early stages. The removal of sap-sucking insects is of prime importance as they are the carriers of viral diseases but should your plant contract a virus then discarding it is the only solution.

### SYMPTOM—LEAF WILT
POSSIBLE CAUSES
*Excessive heat; water logging; drought; high salt content in soil.*

SOLUTIONS
Shade, remove to cooler location; ensure good drainage; discard drainage water; never allow to sit in water; water more frequently; drench and drain the plant several times to flush salt buildup.

### SYMPTOM—YELLOW LEAVES
POSSIBLE CAUSES
*Leaves drop after yellowing: excessive light; low temperature; air pollution.*

*Leaves remain on plant: mineral deficiency; incorrect watering or compost for lime-hating plants.*

SOLUTIONS
Shade plant; increase room temperature;
add liquid feed; water with lime-free
water. Apply sequestered trace elements
or repot in lime-free compost.

## SYMPTOM—WEAK, THIN, SOFT GROWTH
POSSIBLE CAUSES
*Insufficient light; high temperature,*
*especially during the night.*

SOLUTIONS
Increase light intensity; lengthen
time in light; reduce nighttime
temperature.

## SYMPTOM—BROWN LEAF TIPS
POSSIBLE CAUSES
*Dry atmosphere.*

SOLUTIONS
Increase humidity by placing on a pebble
bed; mist regularly with lime-free water.

## SYMPTOM—LEAF CURL AND DROP
POSSIBLE CAUSES
*Wind burn; draughts; too much fertilizer.*

SOLUTIONS
Avoid draughts; drench and drain
plant; dilute fertilizer more; increase
interval between fertilizer applications.

## SYMPTOM—BUD DROP
POSSIBLE CAUSES
*High or low temperature; draughts.*

SOLUTIONS
Adjust temperature to suit; relocate
away from draughts.

## SYMPTOM—FAILURE TO FLOWER
POSSIBLE CAUSES
*Too much fertilizer giving lush growth;*
*immaturity; temperature; moisture*
*content of compost; amount of light.*

SOLUTIONS
Reduce fertilizer or change fertilizer
to increase potassium. Refer to
individual cultural directions.

# PESTS

## common pests

### SYMPTOM—HOLES IN LEAVES
POSSIBLE CAUSES
*Usually insect infestation.*

SOLUTIONS
Clean leaves and whole plant by sponging with soft soap and rinsing with clean water.

### SYMPTOM—HONEYDEW
POSSIBLE CAUSES
*Aphid infestation or scale.*

SOLUTIONS
Clean with soft soap solution and rinse with clean water twice at an interval of seven days.

### SYMPTOM—MOTTLING OF LEAVES
POSSIBLE CAUSES
*Red spider mite if cobwebs present on underside of leaves; mealy bugs.*

SOLUTIONS
Hot, dry conditions encourage red spider mites, so increase humidity. Clean plants with soft soap at ten-day intervals three times.

### SYMPTOM—YELLOWING LEAVES AND LEAF DROP
POSSIBLE CAUSES
*Whitefly.*

SOLUTIONS
Clean leaves with soft soap at five-day intervals at least three times. Use a hand-held vacuum on the underside of the leaves!

### SYMPTOM—STREAKED AND DISTORTED LEAVES WITH SMALL BLACK DOTS
POSSIBLE CAUSES
*Thrips.*

SOLUTIONS
Clean leaves with soft soap at five-day intervals, three times.

# CONCLUSION

*Every home will benefit from the addition of house plants and every grower can reap the undoubted benefits of nurturing and watching plants thrive.*

It is only "in house'" that we can control the environment and provide the right conditions to have a whole world of plants around us, from desert cacti to succulent pineapples, to the fabulous flowers and perfumes of the Orient to feathery fronds of ferns, the amazing bromeliads and elegant palms.

The moment you see that new leaf forming, or the seed you planted emerging from the soil, and you have taken and grown your first cutting, you too will feel the thrill enjoyed by gardeners throughout the world. From then on, discovering the amazing variety of plants with all their quirks will provide years of pleasure.

**PICTURE CREDITS**
Garden Picture Library:
pages 1, 25, 68, 108, 115, 117